All Scripture references taken from the KJV of the Holy Bible, unless otherwise indicated.

DARKNESS & LIGHT: *The Struggle for Your Glory & Honor*

by Dr. Marlene Miles

Freshwater Press 2024

freshwaterpress9@gmail.com

ISBN: 978-1-963164-88-6

Paperback Version

Table of Contents

DARKNESS & LIGHT

Freshwater

Who Is Darkness?

Darkness is complex. It is a place, it is a space, it is a state of mind. Darkness is an entity. It is nothing to play with, or in. Darkness belongs to the *family* of Death. Recall Death was the last thing Jesus had to defeat. He spoke of it in His ministry time here on Earth.

There's a family of Death?

Appears so.

Thanatos in Greek mythology is the personification of Death. *Hypnos* is his twin brother; hypnosis is ungodly sleep. *Nyx* is night; he is the father of *Thanatos*. *Scotus* (*Erebus*, *Erebos*) is **Darkness**. *Moros* is doom. As an aside: For us in the USA, are you surprised that Darkness is called SCOTUS?

Morpheus was part of the *Oneiroi,* who were dream *spirits* That could influence

5

the dreams of *gods* and kings. His brothers would visit the rest of mankind with ungodly dreams.

There are others in this group; there are other *spirits, demons, entities, principalities, rulers,* and probably *wickedness* that associate with *Darkness,* but I wanted to introduce the main players that travel along with *Darkness.*

First Mention

Darkness was on the face of the deep (Genesis 1:2). Darkness, as in the absence of light, had somehow thickened over the Earth, or parts of it. So how did it get over the face of the deep? If God created the Heavens and the Earth and God is Light, where did this *darkness* come from? It stands to reason that if Darkness is part of the family of Death and it was hovering over the face of the Deep, then God, who is Light, would have to step in and create LIFE to counter that condition, to counter any representative of Death, which hovered.

Some commentators say that the Spirit of God hovered over the face of the deep. Were they both present, rather dueling, Darkness and Light? Death and

Life? We know who would win that fight: Light.

After Lucifer had rebelled in Heaven and was cast out, he landed here, on Earth. Darkness refers to the kingdom of Satan. Once he fell to Earth, like lightning, after being kicked out for coveting **power, he began to establish his own** empire, here on this planet. That could explain the Darkness that was over the face of the deep, (Colossians 1:13).

The devil comes not but for to steal, kill, and to destroy. So everything God had already created on Earth, once he got here, the devil had put his hands into it to ruin it, to kill it, to destroy it.

Saints of God, by the time Adam and Eve sinned, God quickly instructed angels to get them out of the Garden before they eat of the Tree of Life and live forever. To counter Death, God had even put a Tree in the Garden of Eden and on that Tree was Life. Anyone who partook of that Tree, took Life into themselves and lived forever.

So, when the devil had sinned in Heaven, did not God also cast him out because in Heaven folks are eternal; they live forever.

The devil was a beautiful and created cherubim and he could have lived in Heaven eternally, but he doesn't have that anymore. He has a set and appointed time, and he knows it. But he is one of those abusive and jealous types who is saying that if he can't have something, then no one should. We can again have eternal life and that is one of the main things the devil wants to destroy for mankind.

Darkness is an entity. Do not ask for it. Do not summon it. Do not converse with it. Do not play with it. **Command it.**

What To Wear

In this world we think darkness is just nighttime--, when the sun goes down. The devil has taken the spookiness and terror off of it, but that's for our deception and destruction. For some, especially those who are both *in* and **of** the world, we think that nighttime is fun time. It's when we don't have to work and the partying starts. The clubbing starts.

We all like to dress well. We like to look nice. If we're going out in the daytime, to work or shop we might choose a certain outfit to wear for that occasion. But if we're going out at night, we might choose something completely different. To determine our outfits, we are constantly looking at the weather, the time of day, and the event that we are attending. We may ask, *Will there be darkness? Will there be light? Where we're going? How much darkness, How much light?* The answers to these questions, ofttimes determines what we may choose to wear.

Light or darkness? We'd do better to know if we are going to a place of Light, or if there will be Darkness. If there is Darkness, then spiritual warfare may be needed. We cannot go places defenseless and foolish. It's far more important than what we choose to wear. If that is all we are thinking about--- our *surface* appearance, then the devil's plan against us has already won. Folks, we have to look ahead, to the devil's end game so we are not defeated.

Saints of God, we shouldn't play up to Darkness and accommodate it. Rather we should desire to get rid of it. How would we do that? Bring the Light. Call for the Light.

In the Book of Exodus, God replied to Pharaoh with the 9th Plague: Darkness over Egypt because hardhearted Pharaoh wouldn't let the people go. Sometimes God's way of making something happen is to not do anything so that which is default will automatically happen. If God doesn't bring the Light, Darkness is the default. That's probably how Plague #9 happened. The purpose of it was to counter the idol *gods* of the sun as the people in Egypt worshipped the sun and upwards of about 2000 idol *gods* as well (Exodus 10:21). That plague was described as *Darkness which may be felt*.

Darkness is an entity; it is tangible, it is heavy, it is scary, and it is real.

Have you ever felt a touch in the night hours, but no one is there, but you--, in or out of the dream? That could be Darkness or any of the entities that travel with it laying its hands on you. Kids are smart enough to be afraid of it, but adults should have a certain respect, and take authority over Darkness, not laugh it off as if it is not a real entity with certain power. Plague #9: Darkness covered all the land of Egypt, and it was so thick that they couldn't even see one another.

All Kinds of Darkness

In the Book of Genesis, God created the heavens and earth, and He said it was good. But by Verse Two of Genesis, Darkness was over the face of the Deep. Darkness was over the face of the Deep so quickly--, even by the second verse.

In the beginning, God created the heaven and the earth, and the earth was without form and void, and darkness was upon the face of the deep, and the Spirit of God moved upon the face of the waters. And God said, let there be light, and there was light.

God is the one who created light, because God *is* Light. And, in so doing, God *turned on the lights.*

Verse 3: And there was light. But in verse 2. The devil had come and brought darkness into the Earth.

There are all kinds of darkness. There's a physical darkness. There's a nighttime darkness. There's a darkness that's the dulling of a man's senses. There is the entity, Darkness which is in the family of Death.

God creates. The devil destroys. God creates Light, He turns on the Lights. The devil turns off lights, bringing Darkness.

God turns the Light back on.

Man sins and re-invites Darkness.

God turns the Light back on by His Amazing Grace.

Man was created in the image and likeness of God, so he should be accustomed to light. He should need light; he should want light. So why would man tolerate darkness even for a moment? Why, if he was made in light, made from light, made for light? Then how can man want, invited, deal or put up with Darkness?

In the Garden of Eden, man was shown something different, and man was made to want that different thing, and that different thing was **sin**. In the light there was holiness, there was no sin. But in Darkness, sin was introduced to man. And you see, sin doesn't always happen in darkness, but a lot of sin does happen in the dark, and deception happens in darkness. Theft can happen in darkness. These are things the devil likes to do, so darkness would be his associate, his friend. Evil exchange can happen in darkness. Killing, murder, all kinds of works of the flesh, they all seem to happen in darkness.

We see then that darkness promotes sin and sin promotes darkness. Sin promotes sin, and darkness promotes darkness.

Unless you have the Holy Spirit, and allow Him to bring you under conviction, if you are a Sinner, if you are in sin, then your flesh will celebrate sin, because flesh likes sin. Flesh likes sinning.

> For I know that in me, that is, in my flesh dwelleth no good thing, for to will is present with me. But how to perform that which is good I find not. (Romans 7:18)

The flesh likes to sin, and it doesn't know it's way out of sin on its own or out of darkness on its own. Darkness is a trap. It can be so thick, so heavy, so obtuse that we don't know which way to turn, so we need God. Amen.

So, in sin and in sinning, the flesh may then begin to crave it, or to run to it. Many may not be yearning for Darkness, but instead, the sin. But the devil has subtly tied Darkness to sin and sin to Darkness. Further, darkness is in the Family of Death and sin leads to death—so the connection is real. The very thing man may crave, sin may come with something and some things that he abhors. Things such as yokes, bondage, iniquity, punishments, Darkness and Death.

Men loved *darkness* rather than
light. (John 3:19)

When the devil has a man trapped in sin, he will convince a man that because it's dark, that nobody can see you and you won't get caught. That idea is either appealing to you or becomes appealing to you by a devilish anointing. There is a certain precipice that once reached, a person may want to continue, even in sin.

Lord, help us all.

Because of what a person is doing, planning to do, or wants to do sometimes in life you may want to be seen. And sometimes you may **not** want to be seen depending on who's running the plan for your day or your night, especially the night. If your flesh is running it, you usually don't want to be seen, at least not seen the <u>whole</u> night. You may want to make an entrance; you may want your outfit to be seen and noticed, but after that, you may try to hide or sneak away--, that is if your flesh is running the night.

In this way the devil tricks you into wanting Darkness and even inviting it. Dear Reader, you have been warned.

It's All the Same

The light and the darkness, are both the same to God. God can see through the Darkness but sometimes man can't. So, whether you are in darkness or light, **you will be seen by God**. But if your flesh is deceived, and often it is, sometimes you may dress a certain way for the darkness, or you may even *undress* for the darkness. Sometimes you may dress for the light to be seen by others and God, because you want to put forth a good image, *right*?

So, which will it be today? Have you decided which will it be *tonight*?

The light and the darkness are all the same to God. But the evil devil convinces you that it's not, and foolish man believes what he wants to believe, because he wants to appease his flesh. The flesh tells you that you will only live once; that's true, your flesh will only live once. The rest of you, your soul and your spirit are eternal.

God created man and gave man glory and honor to wear, and that is what you should be wearing, whether it's day or night, whether it's darkness or light. If you wear your glory and honor and your crown of righteousness you will be well dressed at all times. Saints, if you are adorned in glory, honor, and your crown you will choose your natural outfits to perfection--, every time.

If what you are wearing does not bring glory and honor to God, then who do you think it is glorifying and honoring? Three choices here:

- your flesh,
- the devil, or
- both

LMK. If glory, honor, and your crown are missing, filler- and squatter-demons will try to inhabit your life and soul and they will influence what you wear. You can pretty much tell when a person is under wrong influences by what they are wearing, or in some cases, what they are *not* wearing.

We are crowned by the majestic sovereign ruler of creation. We are crowned with glory and honor. (Psalm 8:5-8)

All of us have been made in God's image and likeness, crowned with glory and honor, and we were given dominion in the Earth. Amen.

Lights On, Lights Off

God turned on the lights. The devil turned out the lights and stripped Adam and Eve of their glory and honor. He started with Eve.

It wasn't until God turned the Light and the lights back on that's when Adam and Eve realized that they were naked. Then they became ashamed. The Word says that Adam and Eve realized that they were naked, and they were ashamed and this was after God came down into the Garden and was looking for them.

The Church at Laodicea was naked but didn't even have enough awareness to know it. Only the devil can convince a person that they are or are not exactly what they are looking at themselves and seeing; he is a master of deception and trickery. Until we get it, though, we don't get it.

It takes the Light of the World to show us our shame, our sin, our evil and our nakedness. Laodicea didn't realize that they were naked until the Book of Revelations. We must not wait until the very end to get the report on whether we were properly attired or embarrassingly and humiliatingly naked.

The devil turns out the lights, and when he did it the very first time, he stripped Adam and Eve of their glory and their honor. Adam and Eve are our ancestors; their blood is still running in us to this day, so the devil took from the entire family of man. Therefore, we must ask ourselves now, what are we wearing? If we don't have glory and honor anymore, what are we wearing?

God turned on the lights and said, **It is good.** Then, man was created, fearfully and wonderfully, beautifully made, a little lower than Elohim.

The devil turned out the lights and told man lie after lie about who he is and who he is not. Why did man believe him? Possibly because he tied the lies to pleasure and the flesh loves pleasure. The devil tied the lies to sex and all other sins that man now craves. Isn't this exactly how brainwashing and enemy interrogations and wartime defections are accomplished?

It is not until the physical, or spiritual lights of our understanding are turned on again that we can even see. This is what that Amazing Grace is about, the Lord has turned on the lights for the sinner.

Looky Looky

The devil comes and turns out the lights.

The devil did something else before he turned out those lights. He trained man to use his natural eyes. He said to Eve, something like, "Look at this tree, look at this fruit, look, look, look." With her natural eyes, she did; and then click. He turned out the lights.

Using our natural eyes we can only see *surface* things. But with the heart, with the spirit of man, we can see everything. But the devil has *untaught* man to look with the spirit, to discern, and to look with his spiritual eyes. And he's taught him to look with his natural eyes, to look on flesh and outward and surface things. This teaching was done by his words and also by devil distraction after flesh distraction, and sin.

Sadly, man has decided to unlearn what he was made and built for, to take the distractions, enter into sin as if sin is a perk or a treat and in so doing, relearn a lie--, Oh, you won't surely die; and then remain in Darkness. Darkness is just one of the Family, but once it arrives it invites the others, either quickly or slowly.

Has Everybody Gone *Surface*?

So, the devil has taught man to look at the surface, and then the devil manipulates the surface of things to look like what he wants those things to look like. Darkness was over the FACE of the deep. The face of a thing, the façade of it, the surface. Darkness was as a veneer, a lamination over the deep. It wasn't through and through the Deep, it was only on the surface. That to me, speaks to how much authority the devil actually has—*surface authority*. Uncontested the devil does have power, but up against God? How can a fallen angel beat God; it can't happen.

The devil can even transform himself into an angel of light. 2 Corinthians 11:14 –

here that means he assumes the *appearance* of someone else as in a masquerade. You see it is all image and façade; it is *surface*.

God is deep. Who can fathom the depths of God? No where in Scripture is Satan described as deep. Even if he were, he has no way to penetrate the depths of God.

> But the Lord said unto Samuel, Look not on his countenance, or on the height of his stature, because I have refused him. For the Lord sees not as man sees. For man looks on the outward appearance, but the Lord looks on the heart. (1 Samuel 16:7)

God has turned the lights on. That's the lights of our spiritual discernment. He's crowned us with glory and honor and given us position and authority in the earth. Amen. Set us in dominion and taught us how to see in the spirit because that is where we should be operating--, in the spirit.

We are spirit beings; we must operate in the spirit. It would not be beneficial or even possible for us to have to operate in the Spirit if we can't see and/or hear in the Spirit.

Obviously, our God-given glory and the crown of honor came with, among other things, the ability to navigate and negotiate in the Spirit, God's way.

The devil, of course, has a counterfeit for that and everything else legitimate that God has. Stay out of devil lanes, they will not get you where you need to go. As a matter of fact, those lanes skew vision and will take you off the path you should be on.

But, if you are just looking at the surface, you could be very content--, deceived, but satisfied, at least temporarily, with what you see, and where you think you are going.

Click!

The devil has come along and said, *Oh, you don't need to see all of that. Look at this. Look at this, look at this, instead.* And, while you are looking, here is some pleasure for your flesh and soul.

God has the lights on and then, click, the devil turns the surface lights out again and man forgot his position while those lights were out. He forgot what he was supposed to be doing and why he was here and how he really functions and how he really works. With the glory gone and the crown gone, certain authorities and abilities were also removed from man. When God breathed in us and made us living souls that came with a lot of perks. When we were ripped off, we became perk-less without even realizing it. Over time, man may have just forgotten how wonderfully he was made. He may just think he's a form of clay like a mannequin in a store window that you hang clothes on. And so not knowing who he is, being bored, looking for something to do, he finds clothes and makeup and preoccupies himself with what to wear. He finds sex. He finds money. Or, that man who is in spiritual darkness finds food, for example, and makes his stomach his *god*.

Now, just like Jesus' Wilderness temptations the devil has set all kinds of worldly and manmade stuff in front of us and said, *Look, Look, Look*. He even did that with Jesus in that third temptation:

Again, the devil took Him up on an exceedingly high mountain, and showed Him all the kingdoms of the world and their glory. And he said to Him, "All these things I will give You if You will fall down and worship me."

Then Jesus said to him, "Away with you, Satan! For it is written, 'You shall worship the LORD your God, and Him only you shall serve.' (Matthew 4:8-10)

God had the lights on. He had paid the utility bill. The electric bill was paid in full. And man was clothed in glory and crowned with honor, looking marvelous. Then the devil turned out the lights and *took the glory*. Or at least, *covered* the glory of mankind, and he also took the crown of honor. He either then made man forget that he had all that, and was *all that*, or man got so distracted with the baubles that the devil didn't even create, and started playing with those physical things, abandoning spiritual things, to his own demise.

Mankind: Earth is a learning ground for spiritual things, not a sandbox for your toys.

That old lights-out trick did not work with Jesus because Jesus looked past the surface and continued to see in the Spirit, Jesus didn't sin, nor did Jesus lose His glory or His crown of honor. Jesus didn't fall for the old okie-doke.

Now, we can ask mankind, *Where is your glory?* Without that glory, man became naked because His glory was his covering. His glory was what he was wearing. Man became naked. However, as long as man is in the dark he either doesn't even know he is naked, or is content to believe that no one else can see his nakedness. The sad part is that once man realizes all he has lost he takes the fight to the flesh world and wars with other humans. He steals from other humans, he lies and kills and will even destroy to try to get back what he really did lose, but the other man didn't steal it from him.

The devil took it.

In the dark.

But so many don't see the devil or even realize that he exists because the devil is a spirit, and our eyes have been tricked to only be near sighted. The devil puts up many surface things for us to look at and if we are not trained to see past that stuff, we get stuck looking at exactly what the devil wants us to see, and only that. If we had spiritual vision we could also be far sighted, but the real key is to be spiritually-sighted. Those superpowers are from God, and they are increased and sharpened by use.

By disuse they go dormant and what is a wonderful, fearfully made creature becomes as a rag doll tossed about here and there, sitting in a sandbox, playing and wondering what's the next meal or snack that he will have. In this state he has become spiritually spineless and is then relegated to do the devil's bidding.

Please don't let that be you.

Therefore take no thought, saying, What shall we eat? or, What shall we drink? or, Wherewithal shall we be clothed?
(Matthew 6:31)

Keep your eyes on spiritual things. Live a fasted life in prayer. Do your spiritual homework and learn while you're here, versus planning to play all the time. In this way, you won't be *that person*, that rag doll.

The saddest part of all this is unless the Gospel has been presented and or preached to the now-rag-doll, by the time these demonic offerings come along a person can be duped because – hey, it's spiritual. And nothing else has been presented to him, so he may think this is the way to go.

Saints of God, the fields are white to harvest; do the work of an evangelist. Introduce Jesus along the way to everyone you meet. So what if they think you are a Jesus *freak*? Sharing what the Lord has done for you is a very nice way of introducing Jesus without sounding condemning, condescending, or being preachy.

If they don't thank you today, they will remember you in Heaven. Hopefully they will not be in hell wishing they had listened, but do the work to save a soul today and everyday. Remember, someone did it for you.

Poverty and Lack

I believe that mankind suffers poverty, insufficiency, and lack too many times and too many times it's **because of having no glory**. Reiterating, I believe man suffers lack when he has no glory.

When a man has lost his glory, he suffers poverty. He could suffer insufficiency, he could suffer lack, or maybe he has *some* glory, but it's not enough glory or it's not enough of the right kind of glory. And that's why we may not realize the whole package that God created us to have--, perhaps if you miss one part of it maybe it all is then gone.

In the glory package are amazing blessings. Among them is restoration and financial abundance, (Joel 2:23-25). When you honor God, He honors you. When you obey God, He honors you. When you bless God, He blesses you.

Surely you have noticed that when a king comes upon the scene people come to see that king; the Magi did for baby Jesus. They come to worship that king. They bring gifts worthy of a king. Those gifts have monetary value. Money and gifts chase after the glory. When a man has lost his fame, glory, or name no one pays him any attention anymore.

> But my God shall supply all your need according to his riches in glory by Christ Jesus.(Philippians 4:19)

Saints of God, I always thought that verse meant that God's riches in Glory were gold and money that He had stacked up in Heaven. I thought that there--, Glory meant a place. No, Glory is a state or a condition. God is full of Glory; His Glory is too great for us to look on and live. And there is a glory that is due man. So, God in His Glory has His

RICHES and man in his glory should also have his riches, abundance, wealth, and et cetera. Man should not be suffering financially, like ever, unless he is under judgment from God. All the things that Jesus turned down in the Wilderness Temptations He was going to get anyway. The same should be true of us, if we do not fall down and worship Satan, then all the things that we are going to get anyway--, we should get. And we get it decently and in order at the appointed time, and from God.

Glory is the splendor, brightness, magnificence and excellence of a thing or person. We glorify God in worship and whomever worships the Lord, He also glorifies. According to God's riches in glory all of our needs should be met. Amen.

Don't Fake It

It is not good to eat much honey, so for men
to search out their own glory is not glory.
And he that have no rule over his own spirit
is like a city that is broken down and without
walls. (Proverbs 25:27)

We can't even put on a fake glory--, well, actually people do put on fake glory, but people, other people with discernment can see through it. God can definitely see through it. Fake glory is surface stuff, it is the stuff of the image-driven life. Only *fake* people would put on fake glory.

If their own spirit is broken down and they have no rule over themselves and their flesh is running the show, whereas they should be using their spirit man to conduct their lives, their flesh is running things we may see a braggart of a person. So, for a man to tell of his own glory is no glory at all. Bragging is so uncool.

Again, I believe that sometimes people don't have money because they have no glory. Money runs to serve the glory. That's why we should be seeking after what God tells us to seek after, not the money. And you make sure you have some glory on you, the glory that's due man. We don't touch God's glory, but the glory that is due man will draw prosperity to you.

He who worships God, God will glorify. And who glorifies God, God will glorify. By virtue of not sinning, and working in the Garden, in Adam's case, man was worshipping God. Adam was glorifying God. Therefore, Adam's man-glory was intact. With one's glory intact one can do all the things that man is created to do. He maintains his honor, position, authority and dominion.

So, God had the lights on; we know this because glory was all over man in the

Garden of Eden. Glory has its own light and light comes with glory. Therefore, in the Garden there was light from Light and there was Light because the Garden was made by God and then the man's light worked synergistically with all the other Lights.

The Garden bowed. The Garden served. The Earth, the land all yielded to the hand and the work of Adam, and he was fruitful and multiplied just as God had commanded him to be. It was worship; there was no sweat or toil, there was neither hardship nor thorns until after the Fall and the judgment was pronounced. All Creation testified of the glory of its Creator and the created was also respected and received the glory and honor that is due man.

Where is your glory, Saints of God, where is your glory? Where is your crown of honor?

...both riches and. Honor come from you, and you reign all over. In your hand is power and light, in your hand is to make great and give strength to all. (1 Chronicles 29:12 NKJV)

Riches and honor come from God. God reigns over everything, and He has within His hand, power and might. He is able to make us great and give us strength. But we must be crowned with our glory and honor. We must be found in our original estate, in our glory and honor. God crowned us because He wanted us to be made in His image and likeness. And we are.

Honor has with it also wealth and riches. So if the devil has stolen your honor, or you've given it away, possibly in the darkness, or Darkness has snatched it from you, see to it that you repent to the Lord and get it back.

God had the lights on. Man was created in God's image and likeness, a little lower than Elohim, and he was crowned with glory and honor. And in that creation, there was nothing missing, nothing broken.

With Natural Eyes

But the devil *untaught* man to function the way God intended that man function. Our God is a God of Wisdom and Understanding; any dumbing down is from the devil and of the Darkness. **To have one's mind darkened is to enter into a** state of being intellectually clouded and in ignorance. The devil willed man to be ignorant even though we were made to have the Mind of Christ. When God created all, including man, Wisdom was there with God.

The devil trained man to see with natural eyes, saying, "Look at this, look at that."

Then he turned out the lights.

Man didn't know that he could still see by discernment because he had learned to rely on natural eyesight, and only look for and at surface, physical things. But we're going to learn today that we can still see by discernment--, by our spirit man.

So, when those lights were out, man either fell asleep or got distracted in sin so the devil was able to take man's glory. What a caper! Is that why he made the Garden go black that day? Or did the Garden go black *after* the sin? Or, simultaneously?

In the Darkness, the devil took man's honor. He took his crown, his position and authority and dominion and everything else that goes with that.

Instead of being dressed in glory, man found himself naked. Instead of honor, man became ashamed. Then man knew he was naked, and he was ashamed.

Gotta Get It Back

Now we stand here, embarking on a long journey to get all that back. But if a man doesn't know what all he's lost, how will he know what to search for, or even where to start looking? How should he know that he needs to battle for it, or how to do warfare for it? Or how to look for it? How will he know if he has everything once he has found some things or some parts of it? If he doesn't even know what he lost, we will need Jesus in this. We'll need the Holy Spirit. Amen.

Man got put out of the Garden thousands of years ago, and has man then gotten used to the Darkness instead of being used to the Light?

Outside the Garden of Eden there's nothing but darkness. And the other people who were never, ever in the Garden have no light. So, we should not be following those people. We should not be doing what they do or really listening to what they say.

Do they have no light? And that means they have no real glory. So when somebody's talking, we can wonder what kind of foolishness are they talking? What are they talking about? All of these things are about what we see with our natural eyes. They are about sight. But we have far more senses than just sight. We have a whole entire spirit man, and that's what we're supposed to be walking by, the Spirit that is the Holy Spirit, directing our spirit man. We should be walking by the Spirit and not by sight so we don't fulfill the lust of the flesh.

Faith is the evidence of things that we hope for. Faith is needed to please God, and faith is not walked out with natural eyes or natural eyesight. Faith is letting your spirit man lead. Faith is letting your spirit man show you, letting your spirit man teach you, lead you, guide you, because he's being led by the Holy Spirit. Amen.

But it's daytime, it's nighttime, it's darkness, it's light, and you might speak it yourself, the classic, *I don't have anything to wear*. And you really don't have anything to wear because you're supposed to be clothed with glory and honor. And nothing can compare to it. Nothing anybody creates, weaves, makes, designs, sews, knits, crochets, whatever people do to make garments. Nothing.

You really don't have anything to wear if you're of God's because you're not supposed to be simply in man-made things. We're not supposed to be wearing counterfeit garments or devil-designed or devil-made outfits. No worldly outfits. But like Cinderella's slipper, that only fit her, the only thing that man is designed to wear and that is designed for men to wear is made by God and it is made for that man, is the glory from God, and it is his crown of honor.

That man who is now finally well dressed and properly *re*-dressed or well-dressed is wearing what God says and what God designed him to wear. Of that man, and to that man, God can easily say, **This is my son in whom I am well pleased.**

That man is wearing his garment of glory and his crown of honor.

No Glory

There are many more crowns than the crown of glory or the crown of honor, but this this book's focus. In the natural, if you keep going from store to store, from mall to mall, or just shopping online, looking for outfits for your own glorification, you will find that all the outfits that are out there were created by other men who probably *also have no glory.*

If you look at the lifestyles of the designers, famous or not, you could easily see that they have no glory, other than man-made glory, so how can they make an outfit of true glory for you? This is not just the blind leading the blind, this is the glory-less trying to put glory on another glory-less person.

Lord, have Mercy on us all.

Peekaboo

The lights are on. The lights are out, Peekaboo. Where'd you go? Where did everybody go? Where did your stuff go? Are you standing in the dark now, not remembering that you can see by discernment?

Do you even know what you lack? Do you even know what's missing? Do you even know what you had in the 1st place before the sin and the darkness set in?

In a dream there was a lady in a long hot pink dress, and I remember the edges of that dress because she was sitting in a seat, in a large school-like auditorium, but she had her two feet propped up on the top of the chair's back in front of her. She began to talk with permission in the middle of this dream, wanting to discuss the wearing of long dresses. She said Jesus was the only person who wore a long robe because He was holy and no one else should wear one. Yet, at the time that she was speaking she was wearing a long, hot pink dress, with scalloped edges.

I'm sharing this because the ideas of men and mankind and women and womenkind and what we should be wearing and what is OK to wear most often is erroneous. It has a *spirit of error* with it. It's ridiculous. So, we need to *hear* also with our spiritual ears.

Tamar was aware that Shelah had grown up, but no arrangements have been made for her to come and marry him. So she changed out of her widows clothing and covered herself with a veil to disguise herself. Then she sat beside the road at the entrance to the village of Enaim which is the road to Timnah.
(Genesis 38:14)

I'm bringing out that passage to put you in Genesis 38; you can go there on your own. Tamar changed out of her widow's outfit into something seductive and she went out to a place where workers of pleasure were standing or near where they would be standing. She went to seduce. She went to *catch*.

Tamar put on a disguise because she didn't want to be recognized by the person that she intended to have sex with, her father-in-law, Judah.

So, we can put on what we want. We can put on what other people say we should put on. We can put on what we *think* we want. We can put on what we think we want to be. But that doesn't make it the right thing.

Recall, also in the Book of Genesis, Joseph, whose dad gave him a coat of many colors. That was a garment of honor. Joseph's brothers schemed and stripped him of that garment. Then the Ishmaelites and the Midianites came through and bought Joseph as a slave. Then they sold him down in Egypt. In essence, they put Joseph in a slave's garment. After that, Potiphar's wife tried to strip Joseph naked. Without spiritual protection, somebody can strip another person naked, in the spiritual and in the natural. Sometimes the natural stripping constitutes a spiritual removal of garment. Sometimes the spiritual stripping occurs first so that the person will be attacked and rendered naked in the natural.

Naked, of course, means no garment; where did your real garment go? A wrong garment is bad enough, but no garment is far worse. Naked spiritually means to bring one to shame.

We thank God that Joseph had spiritual protection, else the tribes of Israel would not have been saved.

If that weren't enough, then Joseph got put into a prisoner's outfit, yet another garment.

All this darkness and all that sin was in that sinful place, Egypt. Joseph is not even the one sinning, but he's the one being downgraded into increasingly worse outfits. So, we see that one can be put on outfits by force that don't belong to us. But every time you put on another garment, it's as though you go *missing* from where you were before.

All that sin happened in Egypt--, that was a land of darkness. The devil was doing evil exchanges and *switch-a-roos*, almost at will. We must all be careful of enemy tactics.

As said, we can put on what we think we should wear. We can put on costumes and masquerades. Or, we can wear what we were originally designed to wear, be careful not to lose it or have it taken from us. We can be adorned in it every day so when the Lord is looking for us, He will be able to find us. And we won't run away or be ashamed.

Can You See Me Now?

We can pretend. Costumes and make up are for pretending. We can pretend, but we can't pretend always. A person may pretend that we are something we *want* to be, you know, faking it until we make it. But really, are we wearing our right garments on any given day?

If in the Spirit, if you're in the wrong garment, you may not get into places, that is through spiritual gates that you should have access to. If you are not in the right garment, or an acceptable garment, will you even be *recognized* by God?

A change of filthy garment was necessary for Joshua the priest. God is particular about what we wear, what we have on and how we present to Him.

> Now Joshua was clothed with filthy garments, and stood before the angel.
>
> And he answered and spake unto those that stood before him, saying, Take away the filthy garments from him. And unto him he said, Behold, I have caused thine iniquity to pass from thee, and I will clothe thee with change of raiment. (Zechariah 3:3-4).

Will you be recognized by anyone? And so, you may ask yourself, **Does God see me**? Will God see me?

Years ago, I used to work in a hotel where everybody had a certain uniform based on what department they worked in. So if I were off work on a particular day and I saw somebody who worked at that hotel, say out shopping or at the mall, but they weren't wearing their uniform, I would barely knew who they were. I'm usually great with faces and names, so it's not like I really forgot who a person was. It wasn't whether they had on a name tag, or not.

It was that I just got used to seeing this person in this kind of uniform, that person in that kind of uniform and I could easily identify them in their uniform, even from a distance. But when they had on a different outfit, I barely recognized them.

It's kind of like that spiritually too.

So, this book is about whether God can recognize you or not. And if He recognizes you, will He acknowledge you and grant you admission, favor, or whatever you are seeking from Him, or whatever has already been promised to you, based on who you are.

In the old days what you wore indicated who you were. Yes, what status and what class of person you were, but also your identity. People did not have driver's licenses back then.

What you look like, what you wear, how you style your hair, your makeup are all factors on whether God will even recognize you.

When idol gods come to inhabit a soul, that is one of the first things they do, they try to influence a makeover. In the movies it looks positive such as the nerd becomes beautiful or sexy. Sometimes the plain person or the bookworm becomes Goth. Make no mistake the demons, devils, and idols in anyone's soul is what is giving them the idea to make themselves over and what to make themselves into. The first thing that happens is usually a change of garment.

Lord do not let us fall for the tricks, traps and tactics of the enemy as he causes, influences, or coerces us to take off our original garments that God gave us to become something, especially something make believe, ungodly, or demonic.

Have you ever noticed the makeovers of celebrities? From musicians to wrestlers, the more outrageous their new appearances are the more attention they get. Do you think God is telling these people to change into these styles that are either super sexy and or demonic looking?

Of course not.

It is the demons in their souls. It is the deal they've made with the devil. Or, it is the deal that their manager/publicists has agreed to with the devil to make them famous, popular and rich.

Are we so easily tricked?

Where's Your Glory?

Do you look like anything that God made you to look like? Do you have your glory? Do you have your honor? Is it gone because of sin? Is it gone because of you wallowing around in darkness? We all need to look at ourselves. Where is our glory?

When God came down in Genesis in the cool of the day looking for Adam and Eve, how do we not know that God wasn't looking for them by their glory? And He couldn't find their glory?

Theres no glory in this place—. God says write the word, Ichabod over the door.

When the Glory leaves that means that God has left. The glory that is due man or an organization such as a church is upheld by God—by God's glory. When that glory is gone, it's gone.

So God said. Adam, where are you?

In the New Testament it says that a woman's long hair is her glory. Years ago I went to my regular hair stylist, but she did a number on my hair one day. It was soooo bad in my opinion. A couple of days later, when I saw my mother, my mother said, *Where is your hair?*

Mom might as well have said to me, *Where is your glory?*

You might even say that to your own child, *Where is your glory? Where is that thing that you are known for that brings you favor or blessings or that thing that God gave you and gave you specifically? Where is your glory?*

I think God may have been saying to this specially-created man, Adam, without your glory, I don't see you.

God is not blind, but Adam could have been right there in the vicinity and God may have been saying, Where is your glory? You look like a facsimile of yourself. For all we know God expects all of *His* to have glory and that is one of the ways He recognizes *His*.

The devil is adept at masquerades and trickery. He can put up a hologram of a person, and if there's a hologram and there's no glory on it, it will be exceedingly obvious that is not a real person, or the person God made. Sometimes in a dream you might see a masquerade. It looks like a person, it looks like a certain person, but there is no light, no shine—no glory on that person, There's no Light. There's Darkness all around them. There's no glory because they're fake.

Samson's hair was taken; that was his glory. That was the thing that made him unique, different, strong. It was a signature that God gave Samson. But after having lost his hair, Samson lost his power and Samson lost his life, right alongside his enemies.

If the enemy is taking your glory, don't think that he won't try to take your life. Most importantly, what do you think the quality of your life will be without your glory? Recall the work and toil curses of Adam that fell on him because of sinning and thereby losing his glory. Losing glory is like losing favor and that is as if a reproach is put on you. All that makes your life more difficult. Get your glory back, quick, fast, and in a hurry, in the Name of Jesus.

The Magnificence of Glory

Moses asked God to show him His glory. God's glory was so great that God had to protect Moses in the cleft of the rock, and only have Moses look on God's glory as God passed by. Still, Moses' request to see God's glory was a better thing to desire to look at than physical toys, baubles, flesh, and other man made constructs, such as money. At least Moses was asking about something Eternal rather than something temporal. That would have been non-essential and non-consequential, anyway–, at least in terms of eternity.

Because the glory of God is magnificent, and if God gave us any piece of what is magnificent, the glory that's due man, you can imagine how beautiful we're supposed to all be. We are created in His image and likeness, so the glory of man must also be something to behold.

No wonder the devil wants it, searches it out, steals it, or tries to steal it from a man, or try to exchange it and sell it to another man—and the sale is usually for the soul of the one trying to buy it.

If the man who is being stolen from doesn't know the value and the magnitude and the magnificence of what was stolen from him, he may never search for it again. He may never seek for it again, and therefore never recover it, in his entire life. That man may wallow around in his flesh and in the party life all of his life, playing with toys in the sandbox called Earth, and never recover the glory and the crown of honor that God gave him.

In the afterlife, God may not recognize that man. Where is his glory? Where's his crown? I pray that is not you, in the Name of Jesus.

Identification Glory

Glory identifies you, and unless you're doing wrong and you don't want to be identified by God, you're just going to leave your glory off or by the wayside or let somebody steal it from you. Are you just not trying to be recognized by God because you want to sin for a season? You'll get lost in that. Don't do it.

When some folks in the Bible, got really real, when they got between a rock and a hard place, they finally got serious and they realized they needed to repent and they need to get real before the Lord. And they wanted God to **see** them. They cried out for God to not only see them, but to locate them, to find them.

Unlike Adam and Eve, in the Garden trying to hide, these people are calling out for God to see them.

Hagar got put out of the house because she was acting up towards Sarah after Abraham sired Ishmael. She and her son, Ishmael are out in the wilderness with no food, nothing. Hagar is out there, crying to the Lord.

Sometimes we're in a bad situation ourselves. We're crying out to God for God to see us. We're looking for the face of God, and for His favor to turn toward us. Lord, see us, See me, especially in our plight or in our sad or unfortunate conditions.

And she called the name of the Lord that spake unto her, Thou God seest me. For she said, Have I also hear looked after him that seeth me? (Genesis 16:13-15)

Did God answer Hagar for Hagar, or did God answer Hagar for the sake of Ishmael? God had a major covenant with Ishamel's dad. No matter how Ishmael got that special grace, he had it by virtue of being Abraham's child and having a little piece of Abraham's glory? Whether God saw Hagar or Ishamel or both, I can't say, but God did answer and saved them both.

You Are Seen

Listen to me. Yes, we need God to see us, but we also need one another ministry. We need people. We need at least somebody to see us, to know we are here, we matter. We need to know someone cares. **Someones** ideally, but at least one someone.

By word of knowledge, some of you have never been seen. You feel invisible. You feel unloved and unimportant. Not necessarily unnecessary because God is with you. But you need people. You need friends. You need honest connections with others.

And I want to say a special prayer for middle children, middle-born children who are raised in families, where maybe the eldest and the baby of the family got all the attention.

God sees you. God has always seen you. Do not fret, for the Lord will make up the difference. Amen.

1. Lord, in the Name of Jesus, I ask for special attention, Grace and favor for middle and ignored children, that they know that You see them and that You are always with them, in the Name of Jesus.
2. Lord, I pray, in the Name of Jesus that You will send divine connections into the lives of my Dear Readers. Send true friends to them, Lord, at least one. Send people of God, men and women of God with no ulterior motives, in the Name of Jesus.
3. Lord, expose and find out all fake friends, false friends, frenemies and folks who mean Your people no good. If these false people have been in the life of your people, for a season to teach hands to battle and fingers to

fight, Lord, expedite. Let those lessons be learned and let all seasons of friendlessness be ended today and quickly, in the Name of Jesus, Amen.

4. Lord, bind up the plans of the enemy to keep Your people alone, lonely, unconnected, unseen, solitary, or unloved, in the Name of Jesus.

5. Lord, put the solitary in families, in the Name of Jesus.

6. And Father, the Love You gave Jesus for us, for all mankind, we know it's still alive in this world. We receive it, we receive it. We receive it, in the Name of Jesus.

7. Lord, we know that sometimes the touch from God that shows that God sees you comes by the Spirit. But yes, it also comes by way of real human beings.

8. Thank You, Lord. Amen. Thank You, Lord Jehovah Rohi, the God who sees me.

Bring Me Out

For the dark and the light are the same to God. So, if you're in sin, which is darkness, God can still see you. If you are in darkness or place of darkness, a land of darkness, a family or workplace of darkness, God can still see you. Jehovah Rohi, the God who sees me.

Ask God if He will bring you out of darkness.

Speak to the Light, command it, and it'll come and scatter the darkness.

Be the light, put the Word of God in you, and **be** the light, in the Name of Jesus.

Having their understanding darkened, being alienated from the life of God through the ignorance that is in them because of the

blindness of their heart, who being passed
feeling, have given themselves over to a
seriousness to work all uncleanness with
greediness. (Ephesians 4:18-25)

Saints of God, when you sin, that's
you putting yourself in darkness. God didn't
sin. There's no sin in God. That's you. God is
Light; He doesn't live in darkness, that's you,
in darkness because of sin.

On Mount Sinai, Moses (Exodus 20:21)
drew near unto the thick darkness where
God was. This was the thick cloud upon the
mount, in which Jehovah was when He
spoke to Moses. The Lord dwelt in the cloud
upon the Mercy-Seat (1 Kings 8:12), the Cloud
of Glory. That is a holy darkness unlike
anything described elsewhere in this book.

Clouds and darkness are round about him.
(Psalms 97:2)

God dwells in thick darkness. I believe
that since God is deep and no one can
fathom the depths of His power, His might,
His understanding, His Grace His Truth, that

is what I believe the author was implying. If he did mean that Jesus certainly cleared it up when He said that God is Light and He said it how many times in the New Testament? There are more than 40 Verses identifying Jesus with Light in the Bible.

> God is light; in him there is no darkness at all. If we claim to have fellowship with him and yet walk in the darkness, we lie and do not live out the truth. But if we walk in the light, as he is in the light, we have fellowship with one another, and the blood of Jesus, his Son, purifies us from all sin.
> (1 John 1:5b-7 NIV)

God is light. There are as many as 600 mentions of *Light* in the Bible. God is Light. Wherever He is, there's Light. He created lights for mankind, the sun and the moon, and the stars. God commands Light, and we should aspire to walk according to the Spirit, walk according to holiness, and **be** the Light yourself so you are not surrounded and encumbered by Darkness.

In God, there's no shadow of turning, which means there's no Darkness in God. He is Light. He changes not from day-to-day.

Every good gift and every perfect gift is from above, and comes down from the Father of Lights, with whom there is no variation or shadow of turning. (James 1:17-18)

Saints of God, Wisdom and Understanding travel together.

Spiritual sight is diminished by sin, that is, when sin enters the picture. We are not supposed to just be using our natural eyes. But in this life, we need to also be using *discernment* and when we see with our hearts, over the face of the deep—that is deeply and not just *surface*, that is called discernment. That's what our spirit man does. We have crowns because God made us to be *kings* in the Earth and the Word says that it is kingly to search out a matter.

Look deeply, saints of God. Search out every matter. Look deeply.

However, if we sin, it diminishes our discernment. It diminishes every gift, every gifting of the Spirit. And if we only see by the flesh will most likely just seek the flesh experiences and only do flesh works, and in so doing we will walk on every mine the devil has put in our path. We will spring every devil trap put in on our pathways.

Lord, forbid.

Once there's sin, the understanding of a man is darkened and there's Darkness again. Darkness and sin travel together. Sin really makes people stupid, whether you realize it or not. Once you are shut off from the Spirit of the Lord, the Spirits of Knowledge and Wisdom, Understanding, Counsel, Might, and the Fear the Lord, the Seven Spirits around the Throne of God are also not available to you. In sin, you're cut off from those Spirits and you're cut off from the presence of God.

After that, lesser *spirits,* dumb *spirits,* idol *gods* and demons enter your life and your soul. Then how are you supposed to be smart, get smarter, and remain smart?

9. Lord, we need you to bring us out of Darkness that we have invited, entered into, tripped into, or iniquity

that we may have inherited, in the Name of Jesus.

Lights Off

God turns on the Light and the devil turns it off. In the dark, the devil can have his way in many different ways. For example, the light and the lights of the night--, the celestial lights are much dimmer than the light of the day, even though God made it all.

In the dim lights of the night, the moon and the stars, the surface things are much easier to manipulate. It's much easier for the devil to deceive a man. It's easier for that sleight of hand. It's easier to make something that's not an opportunity at all, but a temptation—look like an opportunity.

We may hear laments such as, *He looked like a nice guy so I got in his car with him*. Yeah, that was because it was at night. Or, *She looked like a nice girl--*, yeah, until the lights came up.

In addition to all that, the devil and his agents can program the celestial lights; they work with the Triangular Powers especially, to derive a great deal of occultic and witchcraft powers in their spells and charms.

So, if a person is busy, so busy conducting their sin life, when will they pray? *How* will they pray? When will they command the day? When will they command the night and command those celestial bodies that have been made to glorify God and serve mankind? But the elements can be hijacked by the devil and his agents to hurt mankind. This hijacking hurts the elements and the Earth as well. This is why all of Creation is waiting for the sons of God to appear.

Folks, that's us.

Until then, this is a vicious cycle. Unless we do something about it. Unless we do what God has put us here and instructed us to do. So, while we're out playing and having fun and sinning, the devil's constantly working against us. He's not on vacation, he's at the same party you may be at, but he's working the party.

Humans--, we're at the party doing nothing but enjoying or hiding in the dark, risking getting captured by sin and by the devil. If a person is captive, they won't do any of those things that need to be done, commanding the day, the night, the month, the year. Praying. Discerning. Taking authority over their life, sitting in authority and dominion. They won't be working to break out of captivity or helping others break out of captivity because captives don't pray. They can't. They don't praise, They don't worship. They're captive. It is an anomaly if they do, like Paul and Silas, in the prison at midnight. Those two were physical prisoners, but their soul and spirits were free to praise and worship.

Captives have their understanding darkened, and most often do not even realize that they are captives--, so why would they even *want* to pray? It's like being in a cult.

A cult? This isn't a cult, why would I want to leave this nice place?

Many times, a captive can't hear the Words of freedom that are being spoken right into their ears. They can't hear you. They can't read your lips. At least not in the flesh. This is why we need the power of God when we minister to sinners, the lost, and especially captives. That power is to breakthrough to the mind of that captive and jar him or her back to awareness that their surface life is what caused their predicament and they must go deeper. The must go deeper, past the devil's surface and into the things of God. And if this weren't confusing enough already, they must go deeper PAST the Darkness to again reach and see the Light. Power is needed for that.

Even if they have a book knowledge of what a captive is, they do not believe that it is them or that they need words, teaching, ministry, deliverance or help. And that is because spiritual Darkness has enveloped their mind.

We all need God and the power of God to evangelize and deliver the lost. Amen.

Their Darkness encapsulates them, and it may include great trouble, and calamities and they can't figure out what is wrong with their lives. They may begin to see a little light when they realize that they can't sing the song of the Lord or pray because they really are in a strange place in their lives, they really are in a strange land. (Joel 2:20)

The beginning of this revelation for any of us is when we realize that we are sinners and that we need to repent to God. Else, the place of judgment for sin is in Darkness, and or Darkness, alienated from the Light and Life of God. (Job 10:21)

Us Too

Be reminded that Light and darkness are the same to God. And, they're supposed to be the same to us. Yes, to us.

And if I take the wings of the morning, and dwell in the uttermost parts of the sea, even there shall thy hand lead me, and thy right hand shall hold me. If I say, surely the darkness shall cover me, even the night shall be light about me. Yeah, the darkness hideth not from thee, but the night shineth as the day. The darkness and the light are both alike to thee.
(Psalms 139:9-12)

Recapping: There is a spiritual darkness and a physical darkness.

We shouldn't focus so much on the physical darkness, yet our natural eyes do need physical light to see. But our spirit man can see it anytime and anywhere, as long as we are not cursed with spiritual blindness.

> Of a truth it is, that your God is a God of gods, and a Lord of kings, and a revealer of secrets.
> (Daniel 2:47)

The above verse is King Nebuchadnezzar speaking to Daniel and the king recognizing that he lives in a certain obscurity and darkness because he isn't saved, isn't God's and doesn't have the Spirit of God.

In spiritual blindness, it could be broad daylight or anytime, but if you don't have spiritual eyes, spiritual vision, if you don't have eyes to see, what will you see? Selah.

A person could tell you something spiritual right to your face, they could cast a vision, and you may never catch that vision if you don't have *eyes to see*, even if they've made it plain. Or, if you don't have ears to hear you will not hear the vision. This is spiritual blindness. This is a lack of understanding. This is a person, minus the Holy Spirit. It is the spirit of man that is empowered in spiritual matters by the Spirit of God.

And God said, Let us make man in our own image and likeness. Jesus came and said, I do what I see my Father do. So, we're supposed to be following Jesus as He follows the Father. The Holy Spirit is our Guide, the Spirit of Understanding. You're getting this, right?

So, leading us is what the Holy Spirit does; He leads us into all Truth. The Holy Spirit directs the Spirit of man. Therefore, if we're Spirit-led, then the Darkness becomes light to us also. Under these conditions, we are not stopped, delayed, waylaid, deceived, or tricked either into or out of anything.

Thank You, Lord.

God put on the lights, and the devil turns out the lights after the devil has taught us to turn **off** discernment and just look with natural eyes.

10. Lord, in the Name of Jesus, give me spiritual vision so it doesn't matter day or night, but if I'm still Spirit-led, I can see. In the Name of Jesus, I can see all that needs to be seen. Amen.
11. Lord, let me walk by the Spirit so I do not fulfill the lust of the flesh, in the Name of Jesus.

Thank You, Lord.

Lust of the flesh? Yeah, flesh can *lust* at any time, but at night? Yeah, it's off the charts many times at night. At night when the moon is in charge and the stars are winking. *Oh please.* A man can't see himself, or chooses not to see himself, or pretends that others can't see him either. Not even God. He is so deceived.

Darkness is so ripe for sin.

The light and the dark are supposed to be also the same to us as it is to God, and this is called spiritual discernment for us.

And by the Spirit of God leading our spirit, we should be able to see through the veil that the devil presents, or that cloaks the light, so he can put us in darkness. We should be able to see through the devil's tactics, especially past every surface facade. That is, if we have knowledge and apply Wisdom.

Recovery

In sin, willingly or by trickery, if we have lost our glory or our crown, we can get our glory back and we can get our crown back. We can get our honor back, our position, our authority, our dominion. We can recover it all, in the Name of Jesus. Amen.

12. Lord, restore me to my first estate before I or anyone in my bloodline ever sinned against You, in the Name of Jesus.
13. Lord, I repent of every sin for myself, my parents, and my ancestors, in the Name of Jesus.
14. Lord, remove my filthy garment of iniquity and enrobe me again in righteousness,

glory, and honor, in the Name of Jesus. Thank You Lord.

Ask yourself, saints of God, is your spirit man leading you, spiritually? And if your spirit man is leading, what do you think you'll miss? You won't miss anything. You won't miss a beat. You won't miss a thing.

Jesus answered, Are there not 12 hours in the day? If any man walk in the day, he stumble, if not because he see it the light of this world. But if a man walk in the night, he stumbled because there is no light in him.
(John 11:9-16)

If he stumbles, that could mean he physically stumbles, but it could also mean that this man stumbles into sin, and once a man sins, he loses his glory. He loses his crown. He loses Light. And he falls Into Darkness. But if we look very closely at that verse, we see that a man sees in the daytime by Light, but that same man sees in the nighttime, that is in the darkness by the Light that is **in** him.

How can he get that back? We need to come out of Darkness into God's marvelous

Light, and we do that by salvation in Christ Jesus. Amen.

We recover what we've lost to darkness by getting the Light of God IN us, and that is the Holy Spirit. But we must also hear, listen and obey the Holy Spirit, not just *have* the Holy Spirit.

If there's no light in a place, then you need to **be** the light,

> Because you are a chosen generation, you're a royal priesthood, a holy nation, a peculiar people, and you should show forth the praises of Him who called you out of darkness into his marvelous light, which in time past were not a people. That are now the people of God, which had not obtained mercy, but now we have obtained mercy. Thank you, Lord. (1 Peter 29:10).

You are the Light of the world, and you should take the Light into the world. Amen. When there is no power, you BE the HOT SPOT, spiritually speaking.

And the Darkness and the Light are all the same if ye are the Light. And there should be so much Light in you that wherever you are, there is Light. Wherever you go there is Light. You should be a *hotspot* of Light. You are the Light of the world, doing as you see that Jesus did it. Jesus the Way, the Truth and the Light. And Jesus is doing what he saw the Father do. And we're made in the image and likeness of God.

Let there **be** Light. Being means existing. It means that when you leave a place, you should leave some Light there.

You are the light of the world. A city that is set on a hill cannot be hid. Neither do men light a candle and put it under a bushel, but on a Candlestick, and it giveth light unto all that are in the house. And let your light so shine before men, that they may see your good works, and glorify your Father, which is in heaven. (Matthew 5: 4-16)

Even In the Darkness

God can see you, even in the darkness. God can see you in *your* darkness. And that is for the purpose of pulling you out of that darkness, back into His marvelous Light. God turns the Lights on again; thank You, Lord.

Please consider that God never made man for darkness. And He never made Darkness for man, Amen.

The sin of one man puts that man in Darkness. The Bible mentions obscure darkness, and that's really dark. One sin, absent the Mercy of God is enough to kill that one man.

Yes, the dark and the Light are all the same to God, so God can work in the daylight and also in the night. Even in the dark, God can still work and is working.

The sins of **all mankind**, who can fathom that? If the sins of one man can kill that one man, then the sin of **all** mankind would definitely kill a man. Jesus was not blind to that, so when He accepted the *Will* of God, when He accepted the Cup of Sorrows, He had already accepted this impending physical death.

The plan of redemption of sinful man happened in darkness. God is working all the time, even though we are exhorted by Scriptures to work while it is day for the night comes when no man can work. The crucifixion Darkness is an event described in the Synoptic Gospels when, although it was daytime, the sky became dark when Jesus was giving up the Ghost. It was dark for approximately three hours, the time of a prayer watch.

When humans accept sin or choose to sin, we are not wise at all. We think we can cheat death; we think if no humans know that we can get away with sin, as if God is not looking. We carelessly pretend that God doesn't exist when we want to do wrong. We foolishly think that if we sin in the dark, no one will see, as if God can't see in the dark.

> If I say, Surely the darkness shall cover me; even the night shall be light about me. Yea, the darkness hideth not from thee; but the night shineth as the day: the darkness and the light are both alike to thee.
> (Psalm 139:11-12)

Darkness can't rebel against God; He made it, so it must also obey and yield to Him and show Him what is happening within it, even in the pitch darkness of the blackest night.

So, Jesus accepted Death before He was ever nailed to that Cross. He accepted death when He pretty much told Judas to bring it on, since He knew what Judas was doing to Him and that it must be fulfilled.

Darkness covered the land when Jesus hung on the Cross. The Light of the world had died, the devil was celebrating, wouldn't Darkness try to make a comeback? When Jesus hung upon the Cross, from the sixth hour there was darkness over all the land unto the ninth hour.

Saints, this is part of our recovery and restoration. Adam and Eve sinned and then were removed from the Garden before they ate of the Tree of Life and lived forever. They were kept out of Eden by an angel with a flaming sword that turned every which way.

God chooses the foolish things to confound the wise. Jesus hung on that "tree" on Golgotha, and it looked like death. It looked like death had won, but on that "Tree" was Life.

In our restoration, God has provided the Tree of Life again to us: Jesus on the Cross at Calvary is that "Tree of Life" and we are invited to partake so that we again may inherit, experience and have eternal life. There is no angel of God standing against us now. There is no flaming sword pointed at us; we may come freely and freely receive. **AMEN.**

Outer Darkness

Outer Darkness is a term generally used to describe hell or any separation from God. It was not made for man, but it is for sinful, unrepentant man. God never intended to send any man to hell.

But the devil did, and the devil does.

Outer Darkness is where there is weeping and gnashing of teeth. Now, this verse troubles me because as a dentist I see folks who are gnashing their teeth all the time. I prescribe mouth guards and appliances to help mitigate the damage of bruxism or teeth grinding. The problem is, no dentist knows how to make the teeth grinding stop, we only help a person not hurt themselves and their teeth physically for clenching or grinding, gnashing their teeth.

This is the same thing I complain about often that modern medicine doesn't always solve or fix things, we just give crutches and splints—supports to let a person keep doing what they are doing. Botox is purported to help stop teeth clenching and grinding by weakening one of the main jaw muscles and lessening nerve stimulation to cause the gnashing. Note, we said "*help*." Plus, Botox is not permanent, and has to be reinjected periodically two or more times per year.

Botox does not address the **spiritual** reason why people gnash their teeth.

Being uniquely qualified to speak on this, when I look in the mouth I see all kinds of things. The one who is gnashing their teeth is most often in captivity. Every night they are probably trying to get out of captivity. Every night they are having some dream or scenario where they probably *almost* get out of captivity. Every night is tense. Every night is work. Every night in Darkness their soul is in hell even though they are physically still alive.

I am writing about this because I was a teeth grinder and for years went through seasons of teeth grinding. Bruxism, or gnashing of teeth or teeth clenching or grinding I believe is SPIRITUAL. I've reached this conclusion because any medical (or dental) condition that has no physical solution and conclusion is spiritual.

Now, Dear Reader, get yourself a dream and or deliverance journal and write down what you are going through when you get into seasons of grinding, clenching, bruxing, and gnashing your teeth. What are you dreaming on those nights when you wake up the next morning and your jaws are tight like a vice, or you have a foul headache or neck or shoulder pain. What have you been through that night when you woke up the next morning mean, irritable, or exhausted?

Were you trying to break out of a place. Were you being forced to do something or things you didn't want to do? Were you attacked and you were helpless in your dreams?

That is not just outer darkness, it is a serious danger sign. Get out of the devil's prison sooner than later.

Oh, but you're saved. Yes you are. So am I, but there is a problem or more than one problem somewhere and it is up to us to sort out where we came from, what we inherited, what we did, what we didn't yet repent for, what we didn't ask forgiveness for, what we didn't renounce and denounce, what iniquity in the form of demons, devils, curses, and evil covenants from ancestors or evil human agents are holding us captive or pursuing us.

If nothing is pursuing us, then why are we running? Why are we so tired in the mornings? The wicked flee when no man pursueth; we aren't wicked are we? So we must be running from something and trying to break out of somewhere.

Statistics show that more than 50% of the population worldwide grinds their teeth. Most who do it, do it in their sleep and 95% of them have no awareness and will argue with you that they don't.

Hey, God said get married and He has His reasons why. I say get married so your spouse can tell you if you're captive or not and record you if you insist on not believing your marriage partner who sleeps in the same bed with you. Trust this, your spouse will tell you if you do strange or ridiculous things in your sleep. Your spouse will tell you if you talk in your sleep, if you stop breathing as in sleep apnea, and especially if you grind your teeth in your sleep.

Saints, this is proper one-another ministry. It is better than living in the Darkness of Ignorance and night torments for years and years, breaking teeth, damaging TM joints, getting foul headaches, and suffering spiritually in captivity.

You're welcome.

Now, let's pray.

Decrees & Prayers

15. By word of prophecy, I will be thankful all my days on Earth, in the Name of Jesus.
16. By word of prophecy, I shall not die before my time, in the Name of Jesus.
17. By word of prophecy, I shall be successful in Life, in the Name of Jesus.
18. By word of prophecy, I shall not praise idols, in the Name of Jesus.
19. By word of prophecy. I feel and experience the Love and the Peace of God in my life, in the Name of Jesus.
20. By word of prophecy, I set myself holy for Jesus Christ, in the Name of Jesus.
21. By the word of prophecy, I receive the Mercy of God, in the Name of Jesus.

22. By word of prophecy, I will regain my glory, my crown of honor, in the Name of Jesus.

23. By word of prophecy, I receive the favor of God, in the Name of Jesus.

24. By the word of prophecy, I receive redemption of my past mistakes, in the Name of Jesus.

25. By word of prophecy, I shall not commit sin that shall separate me from God, in the Name of Jesus.

26. By word of prophecy and the blood of Jesus I shall cast out all *spirits* of pride in me, in the Name of Jesus.

27. By word of prophecy, I drink the Blood of Jesus, and I'm saved.

28. Lord, have Mercy upon me, a sinner. If I'm none of yours, give me a repentant heart and a Godly sorrow for my sins and make me one of Yours. I believe that Jesus Christ was the Son of God and that He came to Earth and died on the Cross for my sins.

29. I believe that on the third day He was resurrected, and He lives. He lives. I

believe in my heart and I speak with my mouth, I confess with my mouth, and I am saved, in the Name of Jesus, Amen.

30. God, who sees me, Jehovah Rohi, see me now. Locate me now, in the Name of Jesus.

31. Lord, I call for Divine Light and I ask that it flush away all Darkness from my mind, from my heart, from my life and body and my environment, in the Name of Jesus.

32. Lord, let me see myself as I really am so that I'm not surprised like the churches of the Revelation.

33. Lord, the love You gave Jesus Christ for mankind, give it to me, so I'm not loveless like the Church of Ephesus, in the Name of Jesus.

34. Lord, take away any love I have for the world so that I do not fall into the world's traps, as did the church at Pergamos, in the Name of Jesus.

35. Lord, send Your Light and lighten and brighten my Understanding so that I

walk in clear doctrine of Truth, unlike the Church of Thyatira, in the Name of Jesus.

36. Lord, let Holy Ghost Fire entrench us so that we are never lukewarm like the Church of Laodicea, in the Name of Jesus.

37. Lord, restore me to my former glory, to my first estate where you formed me and crowned me with glory and honor, in the Name of Jesus.

38. Lord, give me what to wear, in the Name of Jesus. Lord, give me what to wear, in the Name of Jesus. Lord, I reject all filthy rags; Lord, give me what to wear, in the Name of Jesus.

39. Lord, give me what to wear so that you always recognize me and so that You will be well pleased in me, in the Name of Jesus.

40. Lord, I change out of every false garment, every hateful garment, every garment of rejection, reproach, or jealousy, in any era, age, or timeline, in the Name of Jesus.

41. Lord, restore me to my rightful position, authority and dominion, in the Name of Jesus, to the praise of Your Glory. Amen.

42. Lord, rebuke Darkness, in all of its manifestations, for my sake, in the Name of Jesus.

43. Lord, rebuke all Darkness that surrounds me in all of its manifestations for my sake, in the Name of Jesus.

44. Lord, rebuke the Darkness and all of its evil purposes, in my life, in the Name of Jesus.

45. Lord, rebuke the Darkness and all of its evil assignments in my life, in the Name of Jesus.

46. Lord, I divorce completely and entirely the Family of Death, including Darkness, in the Name of Jesus.

Be ye not unequally yoked together with unbelievers: for what fellowship hath righteousness with unrighteousness? and what communion hath light with darkness?

47. Habitation of Darkness assigned against my home, scatter by Fire, in the Name of Jesus.

And what concord hath Christ with Belial? or what part hath he that believeth with an infidel?

And what agreement hath the temple of God with idols? for ye are the temple of the living God; as God hath said, I will dwell in them, and walk in them; and I will be their God, and they shall be my people.

Wherefore come out from among them, and be ye separate, saith the Lord, and touch not the unclean thing; and I will receive you.
(1 Corinthians 6:14-17)

48. Every arrow of Darkness that has already struck, come out, come out, come out and go back to your sender, in the Name of Jesus.
49. Every arrow of Darkness that has already struck, come out, come out! I

pull you out, come out and go back to your sender, in the Name of Jesus.

50. Every arrow of Darkness that has already struck, Come out, come out! I pull you out, and you go back to sender, in the Name of Jesus.

51. Any power hiding in Darkness, firing arrows at me, I dip those arrows in the Blood of Jesus, and I send them back 7-fold, in the Name of Jesus.

52. Lord, help me to keep my flesh under so it does not invite sin or Darkness into my life in any way, in the Name of Jesus.

53. Thank You, Father. Thank You, Lord, for making me in Your image and likeness.

54. I am fearfully and wonderfully made, in the Name of Jesus.

55. Thank You Father, for making me in Your image and likeness. I am fearfully and wonderfully made, in the Name of Jesus.

56. Father, in the Light or the Darkness, let me see with spiritual eyes. Let me

always with discernment look past the surface and see the inward and the complete picture of any matter, in the Name of Jesus.

57. Both riches and honor come from You, Lord, and You reign over all. In Your hand is power and might. In Your hand is to make great and to give strength to all, in the Name of Jesus.

58. Lord, restore me to real glory, true glory, not fake or counterfeit glory, in the Name of Jesus.

59. Lord, let me not search out my own glory, in the Name of Jesus.

60. Lord, keep me awake from foolishness and foolish and evil disguises, masquerades, and costumes, in the Name of Jesus.

61. Lord, you see me; and you always know that it is I. Lord, help me to keep it real, in the Name of Jesus.

62. Lord, You always know it's me. Help me to keep it real, in the Name of Jesus.

63. I call for the Light, and I command the Darkness to scatter, scatter, scatter, in the Name of Jesus.

64. I call for the Light, and I command the Darkness to scatter, scatter, scatter, in the Name of Jesus.

65. Lord, as You restore me with glory and honor, I thank You, and I bless You for riches and honor, in the power of Your might to restore me, in the Name of Jesus.

66. I command all Darkness to go, go, go! in the Name of Jesus.

67. Thunder of God, roll and destroy every stronghold of Darkness mounted against me, in the Name of Jesus.

68. I bind and cast out any deposit of Darkness, in the Name of Jesus.

69. Every angel of Darkness assisting my household enemies, fall down and die, in the Name of Jesus.

70. I shall not bow down to the powers of Darkness in my household, in the Name of Jesus.
71. Every witchcraft curse that is attacking me from the dark, be exposed, and die, in the Name of Jesus.
72. Thank You Lord for hearing prayers. I count this as done, in the Name of Jesus.
73. I seal this Word, these prayers, these decrees and declarations across every dimension, age, era, and timeline, past present and future to infinity, in the Name of Jesus.
74. I seal them with the Spirit of God and the Blood of Jesus.
75. Any backlash attempted against this Word, this book, these prayers, these decrees, declarations, author and reader, BACKFIRE with reverb into infinity, in the Name of Jesus. **AMEN**

Dear Reader

Thank you for acquiring, reading, and praying this book.

May the Lord turn on the Lights and keep them on, in the Name of Jesus.

May the Lord restore your spiritual vision that He originally designed you to have and may He sharpen your discernment all in the Holy Ghost,

In the Name of Jesus,

Amen.

Dr. Marlene Miles

New Titles:

Love Breaks Your Heart https://a.co/d/1F915AB

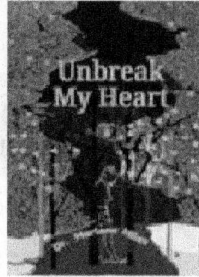

Unbreak My Heart: Don't Let Me Die

https://a.co/d/bH9XAFE

Prayer books by this author

While most books by this author have prayer points either throughout the book or at the end, there are some books that are **only** prayers. You just open up the book and pray. They are listed below:

Prayers Against Barrenness: *For Success in Business and Life*

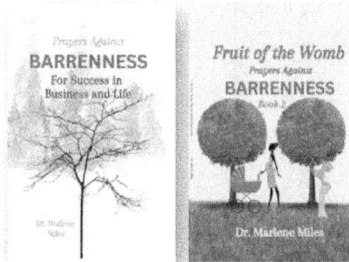

Fruit of the Womb: *Prayers Against Barrenness*

Beauty Curses, *Warfare Prayers Against*
https://a.co/d/5Xlc20M

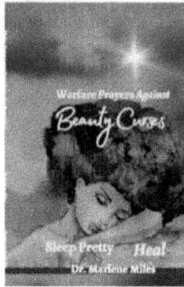

Courts of Marriage: Prayers for Marriage in the Courts of Heaven *(prayerbook)*
https://a.co/d/cNAdgAq

Courtroom Warfare @ Midnight *(prayerbook)*
https://a.co/d/5fc7Qdp

Demonic Cobwebs *(prayerbook)* https://a.co/d/fp9Oa2H

Every Evil Bird https://a.co/d/hF1kh1O

Gates of Thanksgiving

I Call Down Fire https://a.co/d/hN7kGnE

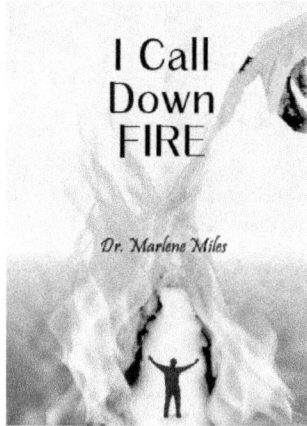

Spirits of Death & the Grave, Pass Over Me and My House https://a.co/d/dS4ewyr

Please note that my name is spelled incorrectly on amazon, but not on the book.

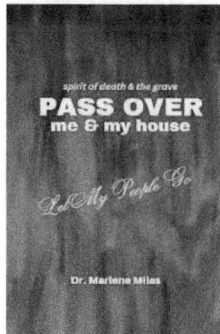

Throne of Grace: Courtroom Prayer

https://a.co/d/fNMxcM9

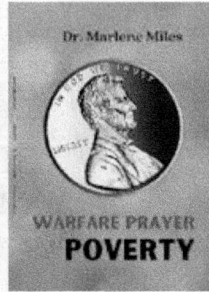

Warfare Prayer Against Poverty
https://a.co/d/bZ611Yu

Other books by this author

AK: *The Adventures of the Agape Kid*

AMONG SOME THIEVES

Ancestral Powers https://a.co/d/9prTyFf

Backstabbers https://a.co/d/gi8iBxf

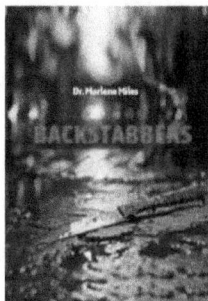

Barrenness, *Prayers Against*
https://a.co/d/feUltIs

Battlefield of Marriage, *The*

Blindsided: *Has the Old Man Bewitched You?*
https://a.co/d/5O2fLLR

Break Free from Collective Captivity

Casting Down Imaginations
https://a.co/d/1UxlLqa

Churchzilla, The Wanna-Be, Supposed-to-be
Bride of Christ

Curses of Blind Men

Darkness & Light

Demonic Cobwebs (prayerbook)

Demonic Time Bombs

Demons Hate Questions

Devil Loves Trauma, *The*

Devil Weapons: Unforgiveness, Bitterness,…

The Devourers: Thieves of Darkness 2

Do Not Swear by the Moon

Don't Refuse Me, Lord (4 book series)

https://a.co/d/idP34LG

Dream Defilement

The Emptiers: *Thieves of Darkness, 1*
https://a.co/d/5I4n5mc

Evil Touch https://a.co/d/gSGGpS1

Failed Assignment https://a.co/d/3CXtjZY

Fantasy Spirit Spouse https://a.co/d/hW7oYbX

FAT Demons (The): *Breaking Demonic Curses*

The Fold (5-book series)

- The Fold (Book 1)
- Name Your Seed (Book 2)
- The Poor Attitudes of Money (3)
- Do Not Orphan Your Seed (4)
- For the Sake of the Gospel (5)
- My Sowing Journal

Gang Ups: Touch Not God's Anointed

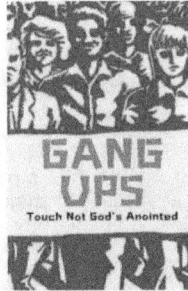

got HEALING? Verses for Life

got LOVE? Verses for Life

got HOPE? Verses for Life

got money? https://a.co/d/g2av41N

How to Dental Assist

How to Dental Assist2: Be Productive, Not Wasteful

I Take It Back

Legacy

Let Me Have A Dollar's Worth
https://a.co/d/h8F8XgE

Level the Playing Field

Living for the NOW of God

Lose My Location https://a.co/d/crD6mV9

Man Safari, *The*

Marriage Ed. Rules of Engagement & Marriage

Made Perfect in Love

Money Hunters: Beware of Those

Money on the Altar https://a.co/d/4EqJ2Nr

Mulberry Tree https://a.co/d/9nR9rRb

Motherboard (The) - *Soul Prosperity Series*

Name Your Seed

Occupy: *Until I Return*

Plantation Souls

Players Gonna Play

Power Money: Nine Times the Tithe

https://a.co/d/gRt41gy

The Power of Wealth *(forthcoming)*

Powers Above

Repent of Visiting Evil Altars
https://a.co/d/fAW2SdK

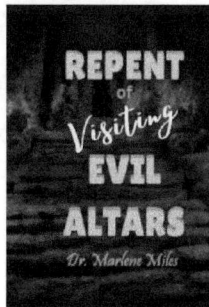

The Robe, Part 1, The Lessons of Joseph

The Robe, Part II, The Lessons of Joseph

Seasons of Grief

Seasons of Waiting

Seasons of War

Second Marriage, Third--, *Any Marriage*

https://a.co/d/6m6GN4N

Sift You Like Wheat

Six Men Short: What Has Happened to all the Men?

Soul Prosperity soul prosperity series 3

https://a.co/d/5p8YvCN

Souls Captivity soul prosperity series 2

The Spirit of Poverty

StarStruck

SUNBLOCK

The Swallowers: *Thieves of Darkness*, 3

Take It Back

This Is NOT That: How to Keep Demons from Coming at You

Time Is of the Essence

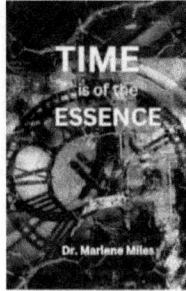

Too Many Wives: *Why You Have Lady Problems*

Tormenting Spirits https://a.co/d/dAogEJf

Toxic Souls

Triangular Power *(series)*

- Powers Above
- SUNBLOCK
- Do Not Swear by the Moon
- STARSTRUCK

Uncontested Doom

Unguarded Hours, *The*

Unseen Life, *The* https://a.co/d/0drZ5Ll

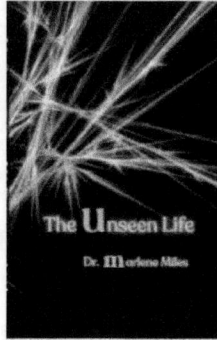

The Unseen Life
Dr. Marlene Miles

Upgrade: How to Get Out of Survival Mode

- Toxic Souls (Book 2 of series)
- Legacy (Book 3 of series)

The Wasters: *Thieves of Darkness*, Bk 2
https://a.co/d/bUvI9Jo

What Have You to Declare? What Do You Have With You from Where You've Been?

When I Was A Child, *I Prayed As a Child*

When the Devourer is Rebuked

https://a.co/d/1HVv8oq

The Wilderness Romance *(series)* This series is about conducting a Godly relationship and marriage with someone who is a Wilderness person. It is about how to recognize it and navigate through it. These books are about how not to get caught up in such.

- *The Social Wilderness*
- *The Sexual Wilderness*
- *The Spiritual Wilderness*

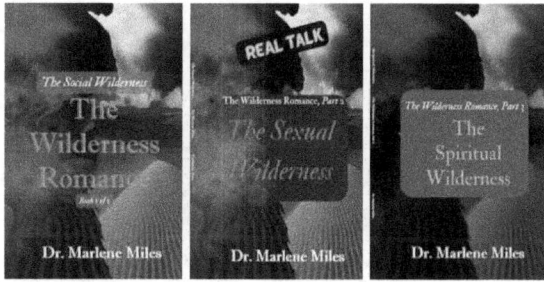

The Social Wilderness
The Wilderness Romance
Book 1 of 3
Dr. Marlene Miles

REAL TALK
The Wilderness Romance, Part 2
The Sexual Wilderness
Dr. Marlene Miles

The Wilderness Romance, Part 3
The Spiritual Wilderness
Dr. Marlene Miles

Other Series

The Fold (a series on Godly finances)
https://a.co/d/4hz3unj

Soul Prosperity Series https://a.co/d/bz2M42q

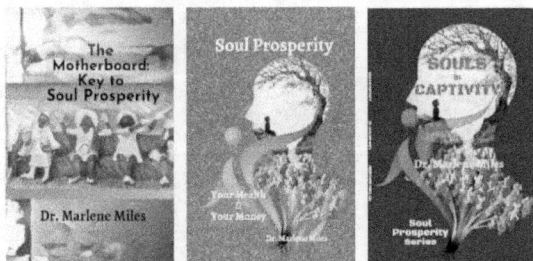

Spirit Spouse books

https://a.co/d/9VehDSo

https://a.co/d/97sKOwm

Thieves of Darkness series

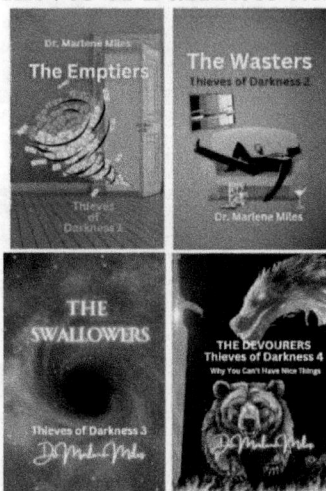

Triangular Powers https://a.co/d/aUCjAWC

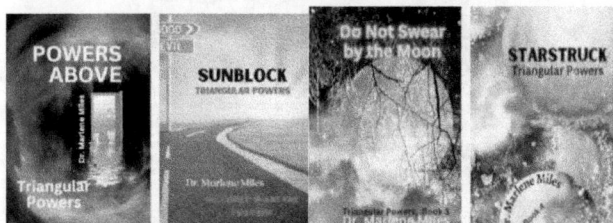

Upgrade (series) *How to Get Out of Survival Mode*
https://a.co/d/aTERhXO

Notes: